# FORTY NARRATIONS REGARDING PRAYERS AND PEACE UPON THE NOBLE PROPHET

صلى الله عليه وسلم

Shaykh Muḥammad Shakūr al-Mayādīnī
*translated by* Yusuf Murray *with a foreword by* Imām Khalid Hussain

KUTUBIC
Birmingham, United Kingdom
www.kutubic.co.uk
contact@kutubic.co.uk

ISBN: 978-1545444504

Printed in association with Suffah Academy (Trindad and Tobago).

# TRANSLITERATION KEY

## CONSONANTS

| | | | | | |
|---|---|---|---|---|---|
| ا | ʾ | ز | z | ق | q |
| ب | b | س | s | ك | k |
| ت | t | ش | sh | ل | l |
| ث | th | ص | ṣ | م | m |
| ج | j | ض | ḍ | ن | n |
| ح | ḥ | ط | ṭ | ه | h |
| خ | kh | ظ | ẓ | و | w |
| د | d | ع | ʿ | ى | y |
| ذ | dh | غ | gh | ة | h / t |
| ر | r | ف | f | ال | al- |

## VOWELS

**Short**

| | | | | | |
|---|---|---|---|---|---|
| ـَ | a | ـِ | i | ـُ | u |

**Long**

| | | | | | |
|---|---|---|---|---|---|
| ـَا | ā | ـِى | ī | ـُو | ū |

**Doubled**

| | | | |
|---|---|---|---|
| ـِىّ | iyy /ī | ـُوّ | uww/i |

**Dipthongs**

| | | | |
|---|---|---|---|
| ـَى | ay | ـَو | aw |

# ACKNOWLEDGEMENTS

The Messenger of Allāh ﷺ said – "whoever has not thanked people has not thanked Allah." I would like to thank the following people for their efforts in making this project possible, may Allāh ﷻ reward them all abundantly.

- Mawlānā Yusuf Murray for undertaking the translation and typesetting of the text at my request.
- Shaykh Tauqir Ishaq for his assistance with the referencing of the narrations within the work.
- Shaykh Khalid Hussain for his encouragement, supplications and support.
- Imām Ansar Francis and Brother Ismail Barton for designing the artwork.
- Imām Kasim Hosein, Mawlānā Muhammad Raza Alam (United Kingdom) & Mawlānā Najibullah Qadiri (India) for proof-reading the work.
- Imām Asif Ali, Hājī Abadeen Mohammed, Brother Feaad Dabiedeen & Hājī Waheed Yacoobali for their contributions.

(Shaykh) Kavir Mohammed
March 2017 / Jamādī al-Ākhir 1438

# FOREWORD BY IMĀM KHALID HUSSAIN

Allāh be praised, who is One and has no partners. High and Sublime is He who has sent forth His chosen Messenger, our liege-lord Muḥammad ﷺ. O' Allāh! Bless Our Master Muḥammad, his family and companions, and those who follow them with goodness thereafter!

What can be more beneficial for all of our needs and requirements in both abodes than sending benedictions and salutations upon the noble Prophet ﷺ? This is the only form of worship we have been given by Allāh ﷻ that will not be rejected - as reported by Ibn Ḥajar al-'Asqalānī in Fatḥ al-Bārī.

We have before us the translation of the text concerning forty Prophetic traditions about sending prayers and blessings upon the Prophet ﷺ compiled by Shaykh Muḥammad Shakūr al-Mayādīnī ؒ and translated by Ustādh Yusuf Murray.

I have read this particular translation and find that herein are those Prophetic traditions that if acted upon and implemented, will bring success in both abodes for the one who does so, Allāh willing.

Let it be known that the Prophet ﷺ has given glad tidings to those who memorize forty narrations, as mentioned in the narration [*ḥadīth*] recorded by Imām Jalāl al-Dīn Suyūṭī ؒ -

"Our Master, 'Abd-Allāh b. 'Abbas ؓ narrates that the

> Prophet ﷺ said 'whomsoever from my nation learns forty narrations, then come the Day of Judgement I will be their intercessor and testify to their faith in the court of Allāh.'"

A similar narration has been recorded by Imam Bayhaqī –

> "Our Master Abū Hurayrah ؓ narrates that the Prophet ﷺ said 'whomsoever from my nation memorises forty narrations which would benefit them in matters of religion, this person will be resurrected amongst the scholars on the Day of Resurrection. A scholar is seventy-degrees superior to a worshipper, and only Allāh knows the difference between these degrees.'"

I pray Allāh ﷻ grants the best of rewards to Shaykh al-Mayādīnī for compiling this treasure, Ustādh Yusuf Murray for translating it and in particular Shaykh Kavir Mohammed of Trinidad and Tobago for initiating this noble task. It is in reality the manifestation of love, adherence and yearning for the chosen one – al-Musṭafā ﷺ – that has brought this excellent project to fruition.

May Allāh make this a form of salvation for us – and not against us – on the day of Judgement, *āmīn*!

*Needy of his Lord and in service of the ummah,*
(Imām) Khalid Hussain
Leicester, United Kingdom
March 2017 / Jamādī al-Ākhir 1438

# TRANSLATOR'S PREFACE

Allāh ﷻ addresses the believers in the Qur'an -

إِنَّ اللَّـهَ وَمَلَائِكَتَهُ يُصَلُّونَ عَلَى النَّبِيِّ ۚ يَا أَيُّهَا الَّذِينَ آمَنُوا صَلُّوا عَلَيْهِ وَسَلِّمُوا تَسْلِيمًا

*"Verily, Allāh and His angels send prayers upon the Prophet. O' you who believe, invoke prayers upon him, and abundant peace."*[1]

In this verse, three types of prayers [*ṣalāh*] are mentioned. Tafsīrāt Aḥmadiyyah mentions that when the prayers of Allāh ﷻ are mentioned in this verse, it refers to His sending mercy upon the Messenger ﷺ. The prayers of the angels meanwhile are prayers of forgiveness, whilst the prayers of the believers are supplications. Similarly, Imām Ṣāwī رحمه الله writes -

> "Allāh invoking prayers refers to such a bestowal of mercy that is intertwined with nobility, whereas the angels' invocation of prayers refers to such a supplication that befits the rank of the Messenger ﷺ."

The author has gathered forty succinct narrations [*ḥadīth*] of the Prophet ﷺ on the innumerable benefits attained and harm both spiritual and material eradicated through the invocation of prayers upon the Messenger of Allāh ﷺ.

1 Qur'ān, 33:56

Without wishing to unnecessarily elongate this work, I consider it important to briefly mention legal rulings and etiquettes related to the invocation of prayers and peace upon the noble Messenger ﷺ.

- If the Messenger ﷺ is mentioned in a gathering, it is compulsory [*wājib*] for all gathered to invoke prayers and peace upon him once.

- Any subsequent mention in the same gathering will only render this invocation praiseworthy [*mustaḥabb*] - one who invokes prayers and peace will be rewarded, yet there is no sin in not invoking prayers and peace.

- When invoking prayers and peace upon the Messenger ﷺ, it is also permissible to include his companions and folk - for example by sending "o' Allāh send prayers and peace upon Muḥammad, his folk and companions".

This practice has its origins in the earliest days of the Muḥammadan nation, and some have said that the invocating of prayers and peace that fails to mention the Prophetic folk is not accepted.

- The scholars have differing opinions regarding the permissibility of sending prayers and peace upon non-Prophets individually.

- If the name of the Messenger ﷺ is heard during the Friday

sermon [*khuṭbah*], it is obligatory [*farḍ*] to invoke prayers and peace silently without producing a sound.

- As the Quranic injunction is unrestricted, so is the legal ruling pertaining to the invocation of prayers and peace. As such, one may invoke prayers and peace upon the Messenger ﷺ at any time - whether he be walking, sitting, standing at any time of the day or night - avoiding places of impurity.

It was indeed a great pleasure to be contacted by my dear brother and colleague, Shaykh Kavir Mohammed requesting me to undertake the translation of this concise but beneficial work on the virtues of invoking prayers and peace upon our Master, the Messenger of Allāh ﷺ.

Throughout the time I have known the Shaykh, I have constantly been aware of his concern for this pristine religion and the *ummah* - particularly those in his country and the geographic and linguistic obstacles they face in accessing reliable and orthodox Islamic literature and academia. I pray that this work goes some way to deepen the love of the Messenger ﷺ in the hearts of the Muslims of Trindad and Tobago and beyond. I further pray that Allāh ﷻ bless and aid all those involved in their efforts to serve the religion and its sacred sciences, granting them ease in their affairs and acceptance in the hearts of the believers, by means of the noble rank of the Elect ﷺ - *āmīn*!

At this point I must also extend my gratitude to my dear brothers and colleagues amongst the students of sacred knowledge who have assisted me in the completion of this work: Mawlānā Amir Madani (Karachi, Pakistan) for his assistance in some linguistic aspects of the work, Mawlānā Najibullah Qadiri (Mumbai, India) and Mawlānā Muhammad Raza Alam (Burton upon Trent, UK) for proof-reading the work and suggesting beneficial amendments and Ḥāfiẓ Faizur Rahman (Chapra, India) for much moral support and encouragement throughout this project.

It goes without saying that any benefit in this work is from the infinite mercy of Allāh ﷻ, and any error is from my own self - I request the reader to inform us of any errors so they may be corrected in future editions.

*The destitute servant of his Lord,*
Yusuf Murray
April 2017 / Rajab 1438

بِسۡمِ ٱللَّهِ ٱلرَّحۡمَٰنِ ٱلرَّحِيمِ

# FORTY NARRATIONS REGARDING PRAYERS AND PEACE UPON THE NOBLE PROPHET ﷺ

## Ḥadīth 1

Our Master Anas b. Mālik ؓ narrated that the Messenger of Allāh ﷺ said -

> "Whoever I am mentioned in front of should send prayers upon me, for whoever invokes a single prayer upon me, Allāh ﷻ sends prayers upon him tenfold."[2]

## Ḥadīth 2

Our Master 'Alī b. Abī Ṭālib ؓ narrates that the Messenger of Allāh ﷺ said -

> "The miser is he in whose presence I am mentioned yet he doesn't invoke prayers upon me."[3]

---

2 Nasā'ī in 'Amal al-Yawm wa al-Laylah (Bāb Thawāb Ṣalāt ala al-Nabī ﷺ)

3 Tirmidhī (3546), Aḥmad, Nasā'ī, Ḥākim & Ibn Ḥibbān

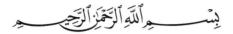

## Ḥadīth 3

Our Master Abū Hurayrah ﷺ narrates that the Messenger of Allāh ﷺ said -

> "May he be spited in whose presence I am mentioned yet he doesn't invoke prayers upon me."[4]

## Ḥadīth 4

Our Master 'Abd al-Raḥmān b. 'Awf ﷺ narrates -

> "The Messenger of Allāh ﷺ set out to drink water, so I also accompanied him. He then faced the qiblah, and prostrated at length until I began to think that Allāh had taken his soul. When I approached him, he raised his head and said 'who is it?' I replied "Abd al-Raḥmān'. He asked 'what is the matter?' and I said 'o' Messenger of Allāh, you remained in prostration for so long I feared Allāh had taken your soul therein.'
>
> He said 'Jibra'īl ﷺ just came to me and gave me the glad tidings that Allāh ﷻ says "whoever invokes prayers upon you, I send prayers upon him, and whoever invokes peace upon you, I send peace upon him." Thus, I prostrated to thank Allāh.'"[5]

---

4 Tirmidhī (3545)

5 Aḥmad, Bayhaqī & Majma' al-Zawā'id (3714)

## Ḥadīth 5

Our Master ʿAbd-Allāh b. ʿAmr b. ʿĀṣ ﵁ narrates -

> "Whoever invokes prayers upon the Prophet ﷺ once, Allāh and His angels send prayers upon him seventy times."[6]

## Ḥadīth 6

Our Master Abū Hurayrah ﵁ narrates that the Messenger of Allāh ﷺ said -

> "Whoever invokes prayers upon me once, Allāh sends prayers upon him tenfold."[7]

## Ḥadīth 7

Our Master ʿAbd-Allāh b. Abī Ṭalḥah ﵁ narrates from his father (﵁) that the Messenger of Allāh ﷺ said -

> "The Messenger of Allāh ﷺ arrived one day with a joyful expression upon his blessed countenance. We (gathered companions) said to him 'we see joy upon your blessed countenance', to which he replied 'Jibra'īl ؑ came to me and said "o' Muḥammad, your Lord says 'does it not please you that if someone prays upon you once, I send prayers upon

6 Aḥmad, Majmaʿ al-Zawā'id (17283)

7 Aḥmad, Muslim (408), Nasā'ī & Tirmidhī

him tenfold, and if someone invokes peace upon you once, I send peace upon him tenfold?"'."[8]

## Ḥadīth 8

Our Master Anas ﷺ narrates that the Messenger of Allāh ﷺ said -

"Verily, there are some angels of Allāh ﷻ who seek the gatherings of remembrance [*dhikr*]; when they find them, they spread their wings over them. They then send their messengers to the heavens and the Divine court.

They submit 'our Lord! We have come from those amongst Your slaves who were exalting Your glory, reciting Your book, sending prayers upon Your Prophet Muḥammad (ﷺ) and beseeching You for (the good of) their hereafter [*ākhirah*] and worldly existence [*dunyā*].'

Thus Allāh ﷻ says 'envelope them in My mercy'. The angels reply 'o' Lord - there is amongst them a sinful individual who merely sits amongst them.' Allāh ﷻ replies 'envelope them in My mercy, for those who sit amongst them are not misfortunate.'"[9]

8 Aḥmad, Nasā'ī (1283) & Ibn Ḥibbān

9 Bazzār & Majma' al-Zawā'id (16769)

## Ḥadīth 9

Our Master Āmir b. Rabī'ah narrates that he heard the Messenger of Allāh ﷺ say in a sermon [*khuṭbah*] -

> "Whoever invokes prayers upon me, the angels do not cease to pray for his forgiveness until he ceases to invoke prayers upon me. Thus, he may decrease in this, or increase."[10]

## Ḥadīth 10

Our Master Abū Burdah b. Nayyār narrates that the Messenger of Allāh ﷺ said -

> "Whoever from my nation invokes a sincere and heartfelt prayer upon me, by means of this Allāh invokes ten prayers upon him, elevates him by ten ranks, writes for him ten good deeds and erases ten sins."[11]

## Ḥadīth 11

Our Master Ubayy b. Ka'b narrates -

> "When one third of the night would pass, the Messenger of Allāh ﷺ would stand and say 'o' people: remember Allāh,

---

10 Aḥmad, Ibn Mājah (907) & Ṭayālisī

11 Nasā'ī in 'Amal al-Yawm wa al-Laylah (Bāb Thawāb Ṣalāt ala al-Nabī ﷺ), Bazzār & Ṭabarānī

remember Allāh. The first trumpet will blow, then the second will follow it, and death with come with all that it entails.'"

Ubayy (b. Ka'b رضي الله عنه) continues "I asked 'o' Messenger of Allāh ﷺ, I invoke plentiful prayers upon you. What portion of my time should I devote to this?' He replied 'as much as you wish'.

I asked 'a quarter of my time?' to which he replied 'as much as you wish, though if it is more than this, it is better for you.'

I then asked 'half of my time?' to which he replied 'as much as you wish, though if it is more than this, it is better.'

I then asked 'two-thirds of my time?' to which he replied 'as much as you wish, though if it is more than this, it is better.'

I said 'I shall devote the entirety (of my time) to invoking prayers upon you' to which he replied 'then it will suffice you (against) your worries and to forgive your sins.'"[12]

## Ḥadīth 12

Muḥammad b. Yaḥyā b. Ḥabbān narrates from his father, who narrates from his father –

12 Tirmidhī (2891), Aḥmad & Ḥākim

"A person said 'o' Messenger of Allāh ﷺ, shall I devote a third (of my time) to invoking prayers upon you?' He replied 'yes, if you wish'. The person then said 'two-thirds?' and he replied 'yes'.

The person then said 'what if the entirety (of my time) is for prayers (upon you)?'

So then Messenger of Allāh ﷺ said 'then Allāh will make this suffice (against) all that troubles you in the matters of your worldly existence and your hereafter.'"[13]

## Ḥadīth 13

Our Master Anas b. Mālik narrated to us, saying - the Messenger of Allāh ﷺ said -

"Whoever invokes a single prayer upon me, Allāh sends ten prayers upon him, erases from him ten sins, and elevates him by ten ranks.'"[14]

## Ḥadīth 14

Our Master Abū Hurayrah ؓ narrates that the Prophet ﷺ said -

"Whoever wishes to obtain reward in its entirety when

13 Ṭabarānī in Kabīr (3574)

14 Aḥmad, Nasā'ī (1297), Ibn Ḥibbān, Ḥākim & Bukhārī in al-Adab al-Mufrad

sending peace upon us folk of the house [*ahl al-bayt*], let him say –

اللَّهُمَّ صَلِّ عَلَى مُحَمَّدٍ النَّبِيِّ وَأَزْوَاجِهِ أُمَّهَاتِ الْمُؤْمِنِينَ وَذُرِّيَّتِهِ
وَأَهْلِ بَيْتِهِ كَمَا صَلَّيْتَ عَلَى آلِ إِبْرَاهِيمَ إِنَّكَ حَمِيدٌ مَجِيدٌ

*allāhumma ṣalli ʿalā muḥammadin in-nabiyyī wa azwājihi ummahāt il-muʾminīn wa dhurriyyatihi wa ahli baytihi kamā ṣallayta ʿalā āli ibrāhīm innaka ḥamīdun majīdun*

'o' Allāh, send prayers upon the Prophet Muḥammad and upon his wives, the mothers of the believers, and his offspring and the folk of his house, as You sent prayers upon Ibrāhīm, verily You are Praised, Majestic.'"[15]

## Ḥadīth 15

ʿAbd al-Raḥmān b. Abī Laylā said –

"I met Kaʿb b. ʿUjrah who said 'shall I give you a gift? The Prophet ﷺ once came to us so we asked "o' Messenger of Allāh, we have learnt how to invoke peace upon you, so how should we invoke prayers upon you?" So he said "say –

اللَّهُمَّ صَلِّ عَلَى مُحَمَّدٍ وَآلِ مُحَمَّدٍ كَمَا صَلَّيْتَ عَلَى آلِ إِبْرَاهِيمَ
إِنَّكَ حَمِيدٌ مَجِيدٌ اللَّهُمَّ بَارِكْ عَلَى مُحَمَّدٍ وَآلِ مُحَمَّدٍ كَمَا بَارَكْتَ
عَلَى آلِ إِبْرَاهِيمَ إِنَّكَ حَمِيدٌ مَجِيدٌ

---

15 Mukhtaṣar Abū Dawūd (943)

*allāhumma ṣalli ʿalā muḥammadin wa āli muḥammadin kamā ṣallayta ʿalā āli ibrāhīm innaka ḥamīdun majīdun allahumma bārik ʿalā muḥammadin wa āli muḥammadin kamā bārakta ʿalā āli ibrāhīm innaka ḥamīdun majīidun*

'o' Allāh, send prayers upon Muḥammad and the family of Muḥammad as You sent prayers upon the family of Ibrāhīm, verily You are Praised, Majestic. O' Allāh, bless Muḥammad and the family of Muḥammad as You blessed the family of Ibrāhīm, verily You are Praised, Majestic.''''''[16]

## Ḥadīth 16

Our Master Abū Saʿīd al-Khudrī ﷺ narrates -

"We once asked 'o' Messenger of Allāh, this is (invoking) peace upon you, but how should we invoke prayers upon you?' So he said 'say -

اللَّهُمَّ صَلِّ عَلَى مُحَمَّدٍ عَبْدِكَ وَرَسُولِكَ كَمَا صَلَّيْتَ عَلَى آلِ إِبْرَاهِيمَ وَبَارِكْ عَلَى مُحَمَّدٍ وَعَلَى آلِ مُحَمَّدٍ كَمَا بَارَكْتَ عَلَى إِبْرَاهِيمَ

*allāhumma ṣalli ʿalā muḥammadin ʿabdika wa rasūlika kamā ṣallayta ʿalā āli ibrāhīm wa bārik ʿalā muḥammadin wa āli muḥammadin kamā bārakta ʿalā ibrāhīm*

16 Fatḥ al-Bārī, Muslim, Nasāʾī, Ibn Mājah, Mukhtaṣar Abū Dawūd (938), Bayhaqī & others

"o' Allāh, send prayers upon Muḥammad, your bondsman and messenger as You sent prayers upon the family of Ibrāhīm and bless Muḥammad and the family of Muḥammad as You blessed Ibrāhīm.'''"[17]

## Ḥadīth 17

Our Master Abū Mas'ūd al-Anṣārī (رضي الله عنه) narrates -

"The Messenger of Allāh ﷺ came to us whilst we were in the gathering of Sa'd b. 'Ubādah. Bashīr b. Sa'd asked him 'Allāh has ordered us to invoke prayers upon you, o' Messenger of Allāh, so how should we invoke prayers upon you?' The Messenger of Allāh ﷺ fell silent, to the extent that we began to wish we had not asked.

Then the Messenger of Allāh ﷺ said 'say -

اللَّهُمَّ صَلِّ عَلَى مُحَمَّدٍ وَعَلَى آلِ مُحَمَّدٍ كَمَا صَلَّيْتَ عَلَى إِبْرَاهِيمَ
وَبَارِكْ عَلَى مُحَمَّدٍ وَعَلَى آلِ مُحَمَّدٍ كَمَا بَارَكْتَ عَلَى آلِ إِبْرَاهِيمَ
فِي الْعَالَمِينَ إِنَّكَ حَمِيدٌ مَجِيدٌ

*allāhumma ṣalli 'alā muḥammadin wa 'alā āli muḥammadin kamā ṣallayta 'alā ibrāhīm wa bārik 'alā muḥammadin wa wa 'alā āli muḥammadin kamā bārakta 'alā āli ibrāhīm fi-l 'ālamīn innaka ḥamīdun majīdun*

"o' Allāh, send prayers upon Muḥammad and upon the

17 Bukhārī (4798), Nasā'ī, Tirmidhī & Bayhaqī

family of Muḥammad, as You sent prayers upon Ibrāhīm. And bless Muḥammad and the family of Muḥammad as You blessed the family Ibrāhīm in the worlds, verily You are Praised, Majestic." And invoking peace upon me is as you have learnt.'"[18]

# Ḥadīth 18

'Amr b. Sulaym narrates that he was informed by Abū Ḥamīd al-Sā'adī  –

"We asked 'o' Messenger of Allāh, how should we invoke prayers upon you?' He replied – 'say –

$$\text{اللَّهُمَّ صَلِّ عَلَى مُحَمَّدٍ وَعَلَى أَزْوَاجِهِ وَذُرِّيَّتِهِ كَمَا بَارَكْتَ عَلَى آلِ إِبْرَاهِيمَ إِنَّكَ حَمِيدٌ مَجِيدٌ}$$

*allāhumma ṣalli 'alā muḥammadin wa 'alā azwājihi wa dhurriyyatihi kamā bārakta 'alā āli ibrāhīm innaka ḥamīdun majīdun*

"O' Allāh, send prayers upon Muḥammad and upon his wives and offspring, as you blessed the family of Ibrāhīm, verily you are Praised, Majestic.'""[19]

---

18    Muslim (405), Abū Dawūd, Nasā'ī, Tirmidhī & Bayhaqī
19    Fatḥ al-Bārī, Muslim, Mukhtaṣar Abū Dawūd (940), Nasā'ī & Ibn Mājah

# Ḥadīth 19

Our Master Ruwayfiʿ b. Thābit ☆ narrates that the Messenger of Allāh ☆ said –

"Whoever invokes prayers upon Muḥammad and then says –

$$اللَّهُمَّ أَنْزِلْهُ الْمَقْعَدَ الْمُقَرَّبَ عِنْدَكَ يَوْمَ الْقِيَامَةِ$$

*allāhumma anzilhu-l maqʿada-l muqarrab ʿindaka yawm al-qiyamati*

'O' Allāh, grant him a position of proximity to You come the Day of Judgement', my intercession [*shafāʿah*] becomes binding [*wājib*] for him."[20]

# Ḥadīth 20

Our Master ʿAbd-Allāh b. Masʿūd ☆ narrates that the Messenger of Allāh ☆ said –

"The nearest people to me come the Day of Judgement will be those who exceed in invoking prayers (upon me)."[21]

# Ḥadīth 21

Our Master Abū Saʿīd al-Khudrī ☆ narrates that the Prophet ☆

---

20    Aḥmad (17454), Bazār & Ṭabarānī in Awsaṭ & Kabīr
21    Tirmidhī (484) & Ibn Ḥibbān

said –

"The Muslim who possesses nothing (to give) as voluntary charity [ṣadaqah] should recite in his supplication [duʿā] –

اَللّٰهُمَّ صَلِّ عَلٰى مُحَمَّدٍ عَبْدِكَ وَرَسُوْلِكَ وَصَلِّ عَلَى الْمُؤْمِنِيْنَ وَالْمُؤْمِنَاتِ وَالْمُسْلِمِيْنَ وَالْمُسْلِمَاتِ

*allāhumma ṣalli ʿalā muḥammadin ʿabdika wa rasūlika wa ṣalli ʿala-l muʾminīn wa-l muʾmināt wa-l muslimīn wa-l muslimāt*

'O' Allāh, send prayers upon Muḥammad, Your bondsman and messenger, and send prayers upon the believing men and women, and the Muslim men and women' for this will be obligatory alms [*zakāh*] for him.'"[22]

## Ḥadīth 22

Our Master Ḥusayn b. ʿAlī ﷺ narrates that the Prophet ﷺ said –

"The one who forgets to invoke prayers upon me when I am mentioned in his presence has forgotten the path to Paradise [*jannah*]."[23]

## Ḥadīth 23

Our Master ʿAbd-Allāh b. ʿAmr al-ʿĀṣ ﷺ narrates that he heard

22 Bukhārī in al-Adab al-Mufrad (640), Ibn Ḥibbān & Abū Yaʿlā

23 Ṭabarānī in Kabīr (2887)

the Prophet ﷺ say -

> "When you hear the caller to pray [*mu'adhdhin*], repeat whatever he says. Then invoke prayers upon me, for whomsoever invokes a single prayer upon me, Allāh sends ten prayers upon him. Then supplicate to Allāh for me (to receive) *al-wasīlah* - for *al-wasīlah* is a rank in Paradise, for a chosen bondsman amongst the bondsmen of Allāh, and I hope that it is me. Thus, I will intercede for whoever asks for al-wasīlah for me."[24]

## Ḥadīth 24

Our Master Abū Dardā' ﷺ narrates that the Prophet ﷺ said -

> "Whomsoever invokes ten prayers upon me in the morning and ten in the night, I will intercede for him come the Day of Judgement."[25]

## Ḥadīth 25

Our Master Abū Hurayrah ﷺ narrates that the Prophet ﷺ said -

> "Whenever any one of you enters the masjid, he should invoke prayers upon the Prophet ﷺ, and say -

24 Muslim (384), Abū Dawūd & Nasā'ī

25 Ṭabarānī in Kabīr & Majma' al-Zawā'id (17022)

اللَّهُمَّ افْتَحْ لِي أَبْوَابَ رَحْمَتِكَ

*allāhumma-ftaḥ lī abwāba raḥmatika*

'O' Allāh, open for me the doors of Your mercy.' And when he leaves the masjid, he should invoke prayers upon the Prophet ﷺ, and say -

اللَّهُمَّ اعْصِمْنِي مِنَ الشَّيْطَانِ

*allāhumma-' ṣimnī min ash-shayṭān*
'O' Allāh, protect me from satan.'"[26]

## Ḥadīth 26

Our Master Aws b. Aws ؓ narrates that the Messenger of Allāh ﷺ said -

> "Verily amongst the most virtuous of your days is the day of Friday [*jumu'ah*], for upon this day Ādam ؑ was born and upon this day his soul was taken. Upon this day the trumpet will be sounded for the second and first times. Thus, increase your invocation of prayers upon me on this day for your prayers are presented to me."

(Our Master Aws ؓ) continues "We asked 'o' Messenger of Allāh ﷺ, how will you recognise our prayers upon you when you have passed away?' He replied 'Allāh has made the

26 Ibn Mājah (773)

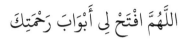

bodies of the Prophets forbidden for the earth.'"[27]

## Ḥadīth 27

Our Master Anas b. Mālik ؓ narrates that the Prophet ﷺ said -

> "Increase your prayers upon me come the day of Friday and the eve of Friday, for whomsoever invokes a single prayer upon me, Allāh sends prayers upon him tenfold."[28]

## Ḥadīth 28

Our Master Abū Umāmah ؓ narrates that the Messenger of Allāh ﷺ said -

> "No one sits in a gathering and rises from it without remembering Allāh or invoking prayers upon the Prophet ﷺ, except that that gathering is a cause of regret."[29]

## Ḥadīth 29

Our Master Abū Hurayrah ؓ narrates that the Prophet ﷺ said -

> "No group sit as a gathering without the remembrance of

---

27 Aḥmad, Abū Dawūd, Nasā'ī, Ibn Mājah (1085), Ibn Ḥibbān, Ḥākim, Bayhaqī, Ibn Khuzaymah & others

28 Bayhaqī (5994)

29 Ṭabarānī in Kabīr (7751)

Allāh therein or the invocation of prayers upon their Prophet except that it becomes a cause of regret. If Allāh wishes, He may punish them, and if He wishes, He may forgive them."[30]

## Ḥadīth 30

Our Master Abū Hurayrah ﷺ narrates that the Prophet ﷺ said -

"No group gather in a gathering without remembering Allāh or invoking prayers upon the Prophet ﷺ except that they will regret the (lost) reward [*thawāb*] come the Day of Judgement - even if they enter Paradise [*jannah*]."[31]

## Ḥadīth 31

Our Master Faḍālah b. 'Ubayd ﷺ said -

"The Messenger once heard a man supplicating in his prayer [*ṣalāh*], without praising Allāh or invoking prayers upon the Prophet ﷺ. The Messenger of Allāh ﷺ said 'you rush, o' one who prays' and taught him (how to pray).

Then the Messenger of Allāh ﷺ heard a man pray, who praised Allāh and invoked prayers upon the Prophet ﷺ, so he ﷺ said 'supplicate, it will be accepted. Seek, it will be

---

30 Aḥmad, Tirmidhī (3380), Ḥākim, Ibn al-Sunnī & Abū Nu'aym

31 Aḥmad (10225), Ibn Ḥibbān & Ḥākim

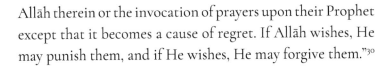

granted.'"[32]

## Ḥadīth 32

Our Master 'Abd-Allāh b. Mas'ūd ﷺ narrates -

"Whenever one of you intends to seek (from Allāh), begin with the exaltation and praise of Allāh as is His due. Then invoke prayers upon the Messenger and then seek. Verily this (method) is more befitting success."[33]

## Ḥadīth 33

Our Master 'Alī b. Abī Ṭālib ﷺ narrates -

"Every supplication [*du'ā*] is suspended until you invoke prayers upon Muḥammad and the family of Muḥammad."[34]

## Ḥadīth 34

Mūsā b. Ṭalḥah narrates than he sought from Zayd b. Khārijah who said that he sought from the Messenger of Allāh ﷺ who said -

"Invoke prayers upon me, and strive in your supplications [*du'ā*] and say -

32 Nasā'ī, Abū Dawūd, Tirmidhī (3476), Ibn Ḥibbān & Bayhaqī

33 Ṭabarānī in Kabīr (8780) & 'Abd al-Razzāq

34 Ṭabarānī in Awsat, Daylamī & Majma' al-Zawā'id (17278)

اللَّهُمَّ صَلِّ عَلَى مُحَمَّدٍ وَعَلَى آلِ مُحَمَّدٍ

*allāhumma ṣalli ʿalā muḥammadin wa ʿalā āli muḥammadin*

'o' Allāh, send prayers upon Muḥammad and the family of Muḥammad.'"[35]

## Ḥadīth 35

Our Master Abū Bakr al-Ṣiddīq  narrates that the Messenger of Allāh  said –

"Make plentiful your invocation of prayers upon me, for Allah has appointed an angel upon my grave. Whenever an individual of my nation [ummah] invokes prayers upon me, this angel says to me 'o' Muḥammad, so and so, the son of so and so has just invoked prayers upon you'."[36]

## Ḥadīth 36

Our Master ʿAbd-Allāh b. Masʿūd  narrates that the Messenger of Allāh  said –

"There are angels of Allāh that roam the earth and deliver the invocations of my nation to me.'[37]

---

35 Aḥmad, Nasāʾī (1292) & others

36 Daylamī (1/1/31) & Kanz al-ʿUmmāl (2181)

37 Aḥmad, Nasāʾī (1282), Ibn Ḥibbān & Dārimī

## Ḥadīth 37

Our Master Abū Hurayrah رضي الله عنه narrates that the Messenger of Allāh ﷺ said -

> "Do not make your homes graves, and do not make my grave a place of folly and celebration. And invoke prayers upon me, for verily your prayers reach me."[38]

## Ḥadīth 38

Our Master Ḥasan b. 'Alī رضي الله عنه narrates that the Messenger of Allāh ﷺ said -

> "Wherever you are, invoke prayers upon me, for your prayers reach me."[39]

## Ḥadīth 39

Our Master Anas b. Mālik رضي الله عنه narrates that the Messenger of Allāh ﷺ said -

> "Whomsoever invokes a single prayer upon me, it is delivered to me, and I invoke prayers upon him, and ten deeds are written for him."[40]

---

38 Aḥmad & Abū Dawūd (2042)

39 Ṭabarānī in Kabīr (2042) & Awsaṭ

40 Ṭabarānī in Awsaṭ & Targhīb wa al-Tarhīb (2572)

## Ḥadīth 40

Our Master Abū Hurayrah ؓ narrates that the Messenger of Allāh ﷺ said -

> "No one invokes peace upon me except that Allāh returns my soul[41] to me so I may return this invocation of peace." [42]

تمت

41 The erudite *ḥadīth*-scholar, Muftī Aḥmad Yār Khān Na'īmī comments on this *ḥadīth*: "'Soul' here refers to focus, as the Messenger ﷺ is now in a state of perpetual life. This ḥadīth in no way means that he ﷺ remains soulless, awaiting someone's invocation of prayers so he may answer them. For if this were true, there are tens of thousands of prayers invoked upon the Messenger ﷺ at any given time - necessitating that his soul be enter and leave his blessed body repeatedly. Note also that the Messenger ﷺ hears and responds to countless individuals' invocation of prayers and peace at any one time. When the Messenger ﷺ is able to hear the prayers of all at once, how then would Allāh be unable to hear the supplications of all at once?"

42 Aḥmad & Abū Dawūd (2041)

23292565R00025

Printed in Great Britain
by Amazon